Inflection Points:
Risk Readiness & Fearless Failure!

by

Tom Casey and Sean Casey

With

Ariana Pazos Aramburú

TP

TELEMACHUS PRESS

Cover designed by Telemachus Press, LLC

Cover art:
Copyright © Color_Brush/iStock/44652960

Published by Telemachus Press, LLC
http://www.telemachuspress.com

Visit the author website:
http://www.discussionpartners.com

ISBN: 978-1-942899-21-1 (eBook)
ISBN: 978-1-942899-22-8 (Paperback)

Version 2015.05.01

10 9 8 7 6 5 4 3 2 1

The trending of an improving economy, coupled with the undeniable turbulence in the workforce, compels leaders to embrace the most generous interpretation of worker and work! Tom Casey and his co-authors, Sean and Ariana, ask the provocative question "Regardless of your age, circumstances or career stage, how do you self-direct the next steps in professional growth?"

Dr. Lynda Gratton—Professor of Management at London Business School Founder of *The Hotspots* Movement and Leader of *The Future of Work Consortium* Author of ***The Shift: The Future of Work Is Already Here!*** and ***The Key: How Corporations Succeed By Solving Toughest Problems***

*The focus of **Inflection Points: Risk Readiness & Fearless Failure!** is timely as Boomers become ready to transition, Generation Xers assume the most key leadership positions in their enterprises, and Millennials accelerate their career choices. I have known Tom Casey for over 25 years, first at Arthur D. Little, and later at The Concours Group, and have come to expect him to ask provocative questions. **Inflection Points** is focused on the common denominators in the making of career decisions for a senior citizen, military officer, and a South American woman. The book makes it clear that one's judgment, supported by his or her personal motivation, can overcome all obstacles.*

Tammy Erickson—(www.tammyerickson.com) Boston Author of a trilogy of books on generations in the workplace including ***What's Next Generation X?***

I am fortunate to work for an organization where the quality of our scholarship and the rigor of our research are what differentiate us in the marketplace. This compels us to hire people from many countries that possess advanced degrees and a plethora of self confidence. The key for our advisors to be successful is to constantly ask the question "What don't I know?" and the motivation to seek the answer. This level of introspection is not age, gender, or intellect driven … it is personal! The book, **Inflection Points,** *promotes the concept that intellectual discipline is an essential attribute of career development.*

Erin Rickards—Chief Human Resource Officer The Eurasia Group, New York

Being a woman executive in Ireland we have to worry about everything today! In addition to the Euro Crisis and worrying about what the Greeks are going to do, we have an obligation to make an impact in our roles. You would think that would be easier than worrying about currency fluctuation, but, unfortunately, it is not. This is because when there is turbulence there is no time for deliberation; there is only time for proactivity. I have worked with Tom Casey for about five years. He came to us at a difficult time and suggested that if one takes risks as a company and/or as an individual, success may not necessarily be guaranteed, however, inertia is its own type of failure. This book will not provide all the answers for career decisions, but you can't help but ask provocative questions.

Carmel Murphy—Director of Human Resources, Arnott's LTD, Dublin, Ireland

It is not often I am asked to comment on a relative's writing, and as this occurrence is likely a one-time never to be repeated event, I felt I should acquiesce. Tom Casey's father and Sean Casey's grandfather was my uncle. He and my father left us at young ages, but with everlasting impressions. They had a simple code influenced by Irish fatalism and periodically understood wit: (1) Be loyal to your family even though you may not be speaking to them at the time, (2) Be supportive of your friends, even if at your expense, and (3) when slammed down by life, get up and say "Is that all you've got?" The book Tommy, Sean, and Ariana (who we have adopted as an Irish niece) have written is powerful in its simplicity ... you own your decisions, you acknowledge your mistakes, and you move on to the next big idea!

Paul Casey—Casey Communications, Seattle Washington
Author of ***Is Self Employment for You?*** and a soon to be
released 10th year revision to this book

I love taking risks! I founded my own firm in a competitive sector of the US economy; I have a pilot's license and balance my professional interests with family matters. The message I identify with most in the book **Inflection Points-Risk Readiness & Fearless Failure!** *is the point Tom, Sean and Ariana make that the unacceptable is when you let circumstances compel decisions, not what you as an individual want to achieve!*

Kathy Freeman Godfrey based in Los Angeles is
Founder and CEO of Kathy Freeman & Co.
(www.kathyfreemanco.com) a Retained Executive Search
firm specializing in the Financial Services Sector

As the recession recedes, all bets are off regarding organizational models of the future, and the requisite proficiencies of leaders. Reflective discourse and dialogue become critical as leaders pursue more responsive and elastic business models. Many think otherwise and live with a reactive, frenetic and rigid organizational model. I have known and worked with Tom Casey for over 10 years. I have gotten used to his willingness to ask difficult questions ... sometimes even diplomatically! **Inflection Points** *is an interesting and timely effort attempting to address, regardless of career stage, the important questions a reflective professional should consider. The authors' compilation of experiences and derived lessons learned are presented with insight and humor.*

Dr. Nicholas Vitalari—Founder of The Elasticity Labs
and Co-Author of ***The Elastic Enterprise: The New Manifesto for Business Revolution***

Purpose of Book
Inflection Points:
Risk Readiness & Fearless Failure!

The authors' objectives in this book promote the following realizations:

- There is no platform for success beyond personal motivation

- There is no predictor for success without risk

- There is no guarantee for success that avoids failure

- The Inflection Point is how one deals with challenges within and beyond their control

Just as important beyond personal motivation are the roles of enterprises and societies in the promotion of self-reflection and channeling of outcomes!

There is no certainty about life, and no guarantee that all aspirations will be achieved, however one thing is certain … it is better to never find yourself in the situation where you ask yourself the question what if?

Notwithstanding the lack of certainty, a higher likelihood of success exists when decisions are characterized by reality, focus, and courage!

As indicated, there is a need for enterprises and societies to engage in reflective discourse regarding the best platform to break down the barriers, which inhibit success.

The ultimate objective of **Inflection Points** *is to encourage the journey, not as some new age venture, but as an expression of emotional intelligence while reminding organizations and societies that promoting reflective discourse is an obligation, not a distraction.*

Tom Casey—Boston
Sean Casey—Philadelphia
Ariana Pazos Aramburú—Lima Peru

Table of Contents

Dedications

My appreciation to my clients, colleagues and family including all of the C's in my life ... nuclear and extended in the US and Peru, and of course the Renners!

Tom

To Gina, and to all the C's and M's in my life. Lastly, and most humbly, to those who have served!

Sean

To the Fantastic Four, my never-ending inspiration!

Ariana

Introduction

Ask yourself this hypothetical question: "If I were to ask a senior citizen, a military officer reentering society, and a young South American woman who is beginning her professional career, what are the *common denominators* among them in how they perceive the challenges and opportunities in career decisions, would their responses be similar?"

You can save yourself time in reading the rest of this book if you presume the *common denominators* are a willingness to take risks, and acknowledgement that potential failure is a consequence of core assumptions.

The authors refer to **Inflection Points** as how one directs his or her career aspirations.

2015 is a turning-point year, one where middle age Baby Boomers reach 65, which was the age when most of their parents left the work force. Those that are still working today, no matter their age ask themselves the question "now what?"

The "now what" question is not limited to those who have achieved Social Security eligibility. It is the all-encompassing question, particularly for those in special circumstances such as a returning veteran or an aspiring South American woman executive.

The questions that are emerging regardless of age and circumstances, or presuming good financial and physical health are similar:

- What is my belief system and will I adhere to its principles?
- What will be my career progression and how will I optimize and showcase my proficiencies?
- What will be my family's and friends perceptions of my sincerity, support, and commitment to their happiness?
- How will I challenge myself spiritually and intellectually?
- Will I make a difference in others' lives and as evaluated by societal standards?
- How will I be remembered by those whom I deem important?

The above is a small sample of the questions that all introspective humans ponder. And, candidly, if we were totally honest, obsess over the answers …

The need for enterprises and societies to engage in the discourse encouraging reflection and channeling the product of self-discovery to promote performance and engagement is as important as self-reflection.

To reinforce this linkage, we utilize three vantage points embedded in this book incorporating diverse demographics, life experiences, and career aspirations.

Sean is a military officer in his early 30s with two combat tours behind him. Wishing to pursue other career opportunities, Sean navigates the world of business communications, just recently completing a master's degree while recovering from post-traumatic stress disorder (PTSD). Sean is involved in veteran advocacy organizations helping others transition from military to civilian lives. Sean is the author of the *Sean Maybe Heard* blog and contributor to the book *Executive Transitions: Plotting the Opportunity*.

The focus of his contribution will be on how returning veterans face the challenges of reentering society.

Ariana is a mid 20s Peruvian national who will be entering a the University of California Berkeley HAAS School of Business MBA program in the fall semester, 2015. She has early career experience as a manager and researcher. The unique challenges she faces, as do her peers in many South American societies, is that they are (a) Male dominated, influencing career opportunities, and (b) the terminal degree for women is unlikely to be an off-shore MBA, both suggesting challenges for decision-making and reentering society post MBA.

The focus of her contribution will be on first party research on the unique challenges facing South American women that aspire to be placed in executive positions.

Tom is now officially a senior citizen attaining the age of 65. His career has been three pronged, not-for-profit management, military officer, and consultant.

He has authored over 300 articles, blogs and four books, including two best sellers, *Talent Readiness: The Future Is Now!* and *Executive Transitions: Plotting The Opportunity!*

The focus of his contribution will be on the challenges older executives are facing regarding transition matters.

Inflection Points:

Risk Readiness & Fearless Failure!

Chapter 1

The Contradiction between
Aging and Clueless
(Tom)

As the recession dissipates and the need for experienced talent resumes, there are two demographic issues that will need to be addressed.

The Need to Embrace the Contribution of the Older Worker

A recent *Wall Street Journal* article spoke of the challenges the legal profession has in maintaining as Partners those over a certain age. The article spoke of a Partner who still practices at 79, who was challenging in court the position of his firm that he was "too old" to fulfill the obligations of being a Partner.

The article went on to speak about his actual productivity (among the highest billing), scholarship (a regular contributor to legal journals and opinion pieces), and reputation as a mentor (younger Partners revere him as a mentor).

So, beyond age … why this dilemma? His legacy firm stipulates that it was being prudent and needs to have a "mandatory retirement age" to make way for "younger Partners."

So, in the legal profession, as is the case in other sectors such as accounting, contribution is not a consideration … the main one is age! Hmmm.

Vitality is not a function of years … it is preparation, outlook, health, and intellectual curiosity …

Speaking of which …

The Need to Understand the Mental Model of the Younger Worker

A recent survey at Beloit College of incoming freshmen had some interesting results. When asked, for example, "Who was Michelangelo?" The response was "a computer virus." I thought this was obtuse until it was explained to me that, in fact, there was a computer virus called Michelangelo.

As a Boomer I thought it would be interesting to create my own quiz and of course answered my own questions as if I was a freshman (I Wish!).

1. What was The Cold War? One fought in the Arctic
2. What was The Long March? The first marathon
3. Who was Beethoven? A dog who starred in 2 movies
4. What was the Kitchen Debate? An argument my parents had
5. What is the Palmer Method? The swing of an old golfer
6. What is a fountain pen? A fountain in the shape of a pen
7. What is pop art? OK this one would be timeless

So, which is more compelling, the answers of the incoming freshmen, or the fact, as a Boomer, I did not know there were two "Michelangelos?"

And more importantly is this an issue of age, intellect, or exposure?

Reconciliation of the Apparent Contradiction

As I was drafting this chapter, I consulted others by Tammy Erickson (www.tammyerickson.com) and my nephew Sean (http://seanmaybeheard.wordpress.com).

In reviewing their writings, the *WSJ* article, the Beloit study, and, most importantly, my pro Sistine Chapel response, I was thinking … maybe this "you lose it with age thing has some merit."

NAAAHHHH!

There are too many aspirations **all who work** have in common:

1. The desire to be respected
2. The desire to be recognized
3. The desire to be mentored
4. The desire to be challenged
5. The desire to be provided opportunity **regardless of age!**

The disconnections we note and laugh about, to the point of cohort mutual mocking, are not a function of age … there are more accurate explanations.

Having given this apparent contradiction some recent thought, I have concluded it is an issue of understanding and tolerance.

Moreover, we will need the energies of all who wish to work to be effective. Therefore, we had best table the ridicule and focus on more understanding and tolerance.

The *Inflection Point* is the belief that the concept of reconciliation between and among age cohorts is a crucial awareness aspect to incorporate into decision-making and as a criterion for evaluation of success.

Chapter 2

Counting The Months to Medicare OR Why I Miss Spiderman!

Recently Tom was up at 4 a.m. for a weekly flight he has to take from Boston to JFK in order to meet with clients. This project has been on-going for about 10 months ...

For those of you who fly to Kennedy via American Airlines, you know once you have landed, you're assaulted by advertisements for Broadway shows ... one of which is *or was* Spiderman!

This ad holds special significance for Tom as his youngest nephew, Pierro, thinks he is Spiderman! This perspective is reinforced constantly by his Peruvian and U.S. family members, who are shameless in buying every conceivable accessory, which reinforces Pierro's image as the sticky savior of New York City.

As Tom was readying himself to wish Pierro a *buenos días*, he realized the sign had been removed and replaced with a mutual fund ad with the caption "In 1960 your life expectancy was 67 ... now it is 78!"

Being 65 and being facile in simple though not complex math, Tom thought, "Oh !@#*, I only have 12 years!"

Not the way for an early morning followed by a long day to kick off!

The rudeness of the reminder of his imminent demise did however prompt him to spend some time online at the Social Security website.

The good news is that according to the website Tom "has" until 84 and a statistical shot at 92 if he puts down the cheeseburger and picks up the salad fork … He hopes the retirement advisors are better at investing than demographics …

In his perusal, he did learn that one was categorically eligible for Medicare when he or she turns 65.

He doesn't know how the rest of you feel, but 65 doesn't feel that old to him. Look at Paul McCartney, Elton John, and the Stones, and think maybe the fact that they don't get Medicare is the reason they keep touring!

Please don't get us wrong, we don't reject the senior discounts at movies, nor, when, in Peru, due to age, we get to go to the front of the line (In the States, this would be the longest line!). But, the aging process does require some adjustments in thinking.

We can't **reject** aging, and when you consider the alternative it is preferable.

We can, however, **reject** feeling old like a watch that is winding down slowly …

Our personal philosophy encourages looking forward, not backward, with the assumption that whatever decisions we made than were considered ... and we have already incorporated lessons learned into how to behave now and in the future ...

Our belief is it is best to look forward to the minutes, days, and years ahead thinking positively and enjoying the ride!

The *Inflection Point* is the realization that life is not determined by actuarial tables, it is the focus of what one does and why, concomitant with the satisfaction of resultant choices.

Case Study:

At 65 Things I Wish I Could Change
(Tom)

I turned 65 in January! For many, many reasons I have nothing but blessings to count!

However, in the perfect world, which I will call "Tommyland," I do have some thoughts on those things I would love to change.

In no particular order this is my bucket list:

- I wish I could walk from the car to the plane without unpacking and having to take off my shoes
- I wish when I get a haircut I could refer to a barber vs. a stylist (I would miss the massages, though)
- I wish I was still ignorant of the dangers of the sun
- I wish cheeseburgers with fries were classified as health food
- I wish in the morning, people hugged vs. tapped iPad's

- I wish other drivers would stop beeping their horns at me
- I wish, when sitting on a plane, I did not need to deflect the back packs heading towards my face (guns and knives are not the only lethal weapons
- I wish when I smile people don't ask me what's wrong
- I wish black and brown could be worn together
- I wish people didn't say "huh" when I mention leisure suits
- I wish remote controls were less complex
- I wish there were only 3 networks to avoid worrying about what is showing on the other 97
- I wish hair follicles were as defiant as body fat
- I wish descriptions between and among draft beers used clearer language
- I wish senior citizens' discounts started at 55, so I would have had more time to enjoy them
- I wish I knew at 35 what I think I know at 65!

They say that 65 is the new 55 ... so I guess I have 10 more years to reflect on how I feel now.

The *Inflection Point* is the realization that a point of view supported by self-introspection is an asset ... a sense of humor may be helpful as well!

Chapter 3

Is Youth Wasted On The Young? (Sean)

*To aid the reader on context, this chapter originates from a blog post published previously. Statistics used are reflective of data available at that time. We felt it would be illustrative to frame a societal reality in the context of **Inflection Points.**

The opening of this chapter may seem pitifully self-centered, but there's big-picture intent. I recently turned 30 years old and came to the reality, whether it's true or conjured in my mind, that I'm no longer a young man. My perception of someone in their thirties was one who would be well into a career, maybe married, own a home, and have a kid or two running around. Depending on your perception of whether it's good or bad, none of these things have occurred yet in my life. While coming to accept that my twenties are behind me, I started to look at the statistics of service members to get a better look at the demographics of our military.

It's become an accepted notion in our society that young people fight wars. This is certainly not unique in our culture. Looking through recorded history, the rank and file of a nation's military had always been composed of young people. However, accepted notions and their meaning can, over time, become lost amongst a people. Let's take a look at the facts.

When looking at Department of Defense statistics, anywhere between 68 and 74 percent of today's service members are 30 years old or younger, depending on the exact branch of the military. An individual must be at least 18 years old or older to enter active service, though he or she may complete initial entry training at 17 years old with permission from a guardian. In 2011, the average age of a U.S. military service member was between 19.6 and 21.9 years old.

So, suffice it to say, the vast majority of people in uniform today joined during the Global War on Terrorism era. These service members never served in a peacetime military. Battles being fought are by people who aren't even old enough to get a break on their car insurance.

Young privates on the ground are often 19 to 23 years old, depending on what age they were when they joined. Sergeants can range anywhere from 22 to 32 years old. Their platoon leaders, lieutenants, are anywhere between 23 and 27 years old since many of them joined right after college. Even the company commanders, captains, range from 28 to 34 years old. Due to the nature of fighting in Iraq and Afghanistan, battles are fought at the squad to company level. The stereotypical general looking at a map with large arrows pointing this way and that can't be found. Critical decisions are being made by young people, people that, when the battle is done, like to go back to camp and unwind by playing Xbox 360.

Based on this quick quantitative analysis above, showing that young people are doing this work, which isn't unique in warfare, let's take a look at the nature of the past 10 years of war our country has witnessed. Operations in Iraq and Afghanistan have solely been undertaken by the U.S. military's all-volunteer force.

Two wars, each lasting over eight years have been handled by those on active duty, National Guard and reserve forces. In 2010, a report indicated there were just over 1.4 million people serving on active duty with approximately 840,000 in some type of reserve component. The U.S. population is a little over 311 million people; so, approximately .8 percent of our population is serving in our military. A service member, depending on his or her branch, will spend anywhere from six to 12 months on a deployment overseas, typically in either Iraq or Afghanistan. Their dwell time, or time back home between deployments, can be anywhere from nine to 15 months. To make things simple in the minds of service members, they accept the fact that, on average, they will spend a year in a combat zone and a year at home.

When looking at these figures one can now see that our current military is composed of very young people spending half or more of their twenties fighting. We realize there's a propensity for older generations to critique the younger ones. I think we've all heard, no matter what your age, the sentence "Well, back in my day ..." Putting your personal views and politics aside, we must realize that there are young people out there doing extraordinary things within the ranks of the military. Their experiences go beyond enduring the hardships of combat. They forego living a carefree and exploratory life, which many people in their twenties enjoy. Some may put off dating, marriage, or school until they're able to enjoy a stable life. Their families and friends endure long periods of stress and anxiety by their absence, which eventually takes a personal toll on the service members themselves.

Many of my close friends who continue to serve haven't reached the milestone of 30 years old, like I have, may not be aware of the talent, dedication, and toughness they demonstrate. These are tools that will serve them well in life. Along with age, reflection will come to them eventually. When they piece together their personal story, I hope they'll realize their youth was certainly not wasted.

The *Inflection Point* is that our culture will once again be infused with warrior citizens who've developed talents, such as teamwork, critical thinking and adaptability, throughout their early professional experiences in the military. An office cubicle and a Bradley Fighting Vehicle are on the opposite ends of the work environment spectrum, yet they're both workplaces. Never discount your past experiences; rather, use them as much as possible. They are an investment you can cash in on in a new environment. Soft skills are one-size-fits-all.

Case Study

In Praise of the Youngest
OR Count Yourself Lucky!
(Tom)

Over the holidays my wife and I enjoyed a long overdue dinner with family members. We had just returned from a cruise, and during the dinner I suddenly realized this was not my 'first' as I had erroneously been communicating.

In point of fact, I had been on a family cruise 50 years ago. I had forgotten. This was not an issue of repressed memory or trauma. Well, maybe a little trauma!

The catalyst for recollection was the dinner discussion regarding family sequence, oldest child, middle child, and youngest child.

Two of us at the table were the "oldest" and our spouses "middle." Accordingly, we thought it only fair to be hypercritical of the benefits derived from being the youngest.

So what does this have to do with a cruise 50 years ago?

During the cruise we had a respite in a Canadian resort. The young staff members there referred to the guests as 'the newlyweds, the nearly dead, and the overfed.'

Being invaded by an American Irish family of seven children, with a particularly gregarious and loud father, but a tolerant mother, would normally be disruptive.

And it was for the guests. But the wait staff and others went out of their way to be assigned to us because we were fun! Granted, based on observation their definition of "fun" may be described as us having a pulse …

But back to the topic of this opus … the benefits of being the youngest.

During our stay at the resort, our four-year-old sister thought it would be a brilliant idea to pretend to disappear. This prompted a search of the hotel, the waterline, and so forth, by family members, hotel staff, etc.

We eventually found our princess hiding under the bed, all the while thinking this attention was just fantastic!

What struck me at the time, beyond universal relief, was the lack of recrimination directed at her by our parents. Notwithstanding some minor "don't you ever" sentiments, I thought if it had not been her, the associated punishment would have bordered on capital!

Years later, as I was entering the military, I asked my father, who was the youngest in his family, why the difference?

His response was "I can speak from experience, the younger you are in most if not all families the more tolerant are the parents."

Of course, in his family he was the youngest! The oldest in his family once admonished her daughter, "You were born into the number one slot in the family. Your siblings will spend the rest of their lives trying to get there."

I have always appreciated the wisdom of my aunt and cousin.

So my conclusion remains … "timing IS everything."

For those of you who are the oldest, I feel your pain!

For the middle child, I would concur, you are often overlooked. However, suck it up. If you are looking for adoration, download Paul Simon's *Slip Slidin' Away* because often you are pardoned, as well!

For those of you who are the youngest … don't venture too far out on the ice when it is sunny! You also can be surprised by timing! Cute isn't everything!

In closing, I want to return to the story of my youngest sister. She was always quiet; we often had to make sure she was not left behind in restaurants, hotels, etc. given the disadvantage she suffered having 6 older siblings.

At given times each of us was assigned the task of 'not forgetting your sister' by our parents.

On one occasion she did, however, slip away and was later found in the dressing room of the Four Seasons, sitting in Frankie Valli's lap, explaining how he should comb his hair.

As one of my brother's once said … "Often forgotten … but never lost."

The *Inflection Point* is the realization that family orientation is THE essential foundation for decision-making. The direction that can be provided can be useful or less than ... the key is to recognize that your choices are YOUR CHOICES!

Chapter 4

Our Own Worst Enemy
(Ariana)

For the past months, I've been attending rehab sessions three times a week to strengthen the upper muscles of my left leg, weakened as a result of extensive bed rest after a knee surgery I underwent last year. Since it was the second operation on my left knee in the past few years, the muscles of my left leg have lost considerable strength; this has become a vicious cycle, as my knee, which has only one-half of its meniscus left, is forced to support a much larger portion of my body weight than it is prepared to. Please note: I am not attending my own 'pity party.' I plan to use my condition as a foundation for making an important enterprise commentary about gender bias in my country and representative of circumstances in other societies which tolerate if not encourage a "glass ceiling."

A couple of days ago, as I lay down on a treatment table while strong electric current was going through my left leg, I realized my ongoing experience with a debilitated knee could somehow help me reflect upon what it means to be a female executive in Peru. How? Simple. The anatomy of human beings includes two legs with which we walk, run, swim, hike and perform all kinds of activities. We, instinctively, use both legs, in tandem, from childhood and beyond. As I have experienced, if there is a problem with one leg, one might experience difficulties. Imagine, for example, driving or attempting to climb stairs to change a light bulb with a cast on one leg. We never think of our dexterity until it is restrained.

Legs exist as a pair to potentiate their own and the other's performance. In the same way, one should wonder: How is it that women, a group that represents half of Peru's population, still comprise a long overlooked vital resource of talent in our society? How is it that we pretend to be competitive and thrive as a country when we are intentionally leaving one leg behind and thus underutilizing invaluable talent?

One can currently find women described in academic papers as the "next and largest emerging market in the world" and the "Third Billion"i, a reference to the expected impact of women in the global economy over the next decade. We focus on considerations in China and India while ignoring the opportunities represented by gender. This "Third Billion" represents an enormous economic resource that must be tapped in order to propel global economic growth. As nearly a billion women enter the economy, not only as workers but also as consumers, new markets are created, and the global pool of talent grows significantly. As a result, productivity and efficiency are enhanced and sustained economic growth is obtained.

Some people might argue that women are already immersed in the global economy, but while notable progress has been made in the past years, there is still a long way ahead in order to achieve gender equality when it comes to participation in the political and corporate spectrums of society. Nowadays, even though participation of women in the corporate world has increased, the more senior the position, the lower the percentage of women we find. There is an alarmingly low percentage of women filling the highest leadership roles in the corporate and political world in both developed and developing economies. More alarmingly so, "Women represent more than half of the graduates in most of the developed world, yet account for only eleven percent of board members, on average."[ii] The representation of women CEOs of Fortune 500 companies is even slighter, at just four percent.

So what is missing? How is it that this amazing "Third Billion" potential is unable to make it to leadership positions? There is a wide gap between potentiality and reality. Let's not settle with what the reality is and start working towards what it could be! Several studies indicate a strong correlation between organizations where women hold top executive positions and improved performance indicators, such as operating and financial results. So why is the incorporation of women into top executive and management positions taking so long?

As in the rest of the world, women in Perú have achieved much progress in the past years, but their access to decision-making in leadership roles is still limited. While considerable levels of gender equality have been achieved in the education and health fronts, marked inequalities in economic and political issues still prevail, and an evident gender bias is evidenced as we analyze leadership roles in organizations.

Revising just a few concerning facts about the current situation in Perú, in The Global Gender Gap Report (2013) by the World Economic Forum, Perú is situated, in terms of gender equality, in the 80th position (out of 136 countries), while it was ranked in 44th place just four years before, in 2009. Furthermore, the percentage of firms with female top managers is just 14 percent, and this statistic becomes even more alarming as we find a mere six percent of board seats in listed companies occupied by women.

Clearly, access for women to political and corporate leadership positions in Perú is very limited, which leads to the mean income of women representing just 65 percent of that of men.[iii] So, what are the main challenges and barriers women face in Perú, which are keeping them from assuming critical leadership roles in society? Why are there so few women top executives in Perú?

There are several stringent social and cultural restrictions, such as gender stereotypes, which are the main cause behind the alarming gap between the access of men and women to power positions. Gender stereotypes portray men as action oriented, competent, confident, assertive and driven, characteristics socially associated with resource control and power. Women, on the other hand, are associated with the so called 'soft skills.' Women and men assume their different social roles from an early stage, and their behavior is shaped by the social norms that dictate what they are and what they should be. As society tends to react negatively to deviations in social roles of women and men, a problematic issue arises in the access of women to leadership positions: If they behave as leaders, they are perceived as failing in their female roles, and if they behave as women, they are perceived as incompetent leaders.

Female executives interviewed agreed that "when women leaders are driven and action oriented in leadership roles, they are largely perceived as aggressive; while, on the other hand, action oriented men are perceived as energetic."[iv] These perceptions must be changed! Society must embrace the competitive advantage of female competencies in order to see the amazing talent they can bring to the table as an asset and not a liability. Organizational cultures may be acting as filters in the access of women to leadership positions, where only people with certain characteristics resembling those on top (mostly men) are considered to assume leadership roles. But in a critical environment of economic deceleration, organizations must challenge existing approaches and think differently to encourage fresh viewpoints and solutions that challenge the status quo. We must bring diversity to the table. A lack of diversity in the corporate and political worlds excludes ideas, thoughts, and perspectives, and thus an enormous opportunity to succeed is lost. Diversity leads to fresh and robust solutions, driven by more informed decision-making and innovation as it leverages individual skills and perspectives.

Is Perú missing an opportunity? Clearly. Should Perú harness the intellect and energy of its female talent more aggressively? Definitely. So, what can be done to improve the situation? First of all, we cannot ignore the problem. We need a society sensitive to the importance and complexity of gender inequality issues. We need a country that fosters a social and economic environment that promotes equal education, training, and professional development opportunities for men and women. We need programs within organizations to help both men and women grow professionally based on meritocracy, and we need equal pay for professionals holding equivalent positions. We need commitment from senior leaders towards gender equality in order to reach transformational change. We need a community of successful women building strong relationships and connections with each other. Perú has a long way to go in order to achieve transformational change in inclusiveness and gender equality, and it should be sustained as a national priority.

Leaving aside the fact that providing equal opportunities for men and women is "the right thing to do," there are significant and proven economic benefits of empowering women, and we should fiercely capitalize on this overlooked pool of talent and skills. Given the complex challenges ahead, if half of the population is left behind, we are missing an important part of the solution. If Perú is to stay competitive worldwide, we must foster inclusiveness to ensure that women and men get the same opportunities to reach their full potential. Capitalizing on the underutilized potential of women is a strategic imperative!

The *Inflection Point* is the awareness that societal norms are in and of themselves often challenging. Granted we are using Peru as an example, but the "glass ceiling" is alive and well in many societies. Our hypothesis is that assertive risk taking, regardless of level of support, is the provenance of the individual and self-accountability the foundation for success.

Case Study:

Pilobolus … A Collaborative Nirvana!
(Tom)

The term Pilobolus refers to a fungus whose spores propel with extraordinary speed, accuracy, and strength … it is also a creative dance company founded by Dartmouth College students in 1971.

The Dance Company has survived and prospered on a global scale for 45 years incorporating innovation, education, and creativity!

My wife and I attend many dance company presentations from ballet through modern platforms. Yet the recent performance of this troupe in Boston was unlike any we have ever seen.

The degree of collaborative precision and feats of strength were magnificent to behold.

The six dancers are incredibly strong and flexible. Audience emotions range from envious wondering how come one's three times a month visit to the gym for 30 minutes does not produce a similar outcome. In addition, but certainly not least, one sits in wonder questioning whether or not the dancers' skeletal frameworks are calcium or silly putty based.

Unusual for us, we decided to stay to participate in the cast post performance Q&A.

The conclusion we drew, and the derived lessons learned for commercial enterprises, were three-fold.

1. Each member of the company was encouraged to contribute to the choreography process regardless of tenure or role ... it is not a "leader led" organization
2. Each member of the company felt a degree of ownership due to this approach, therefore raising their already high level of accountability for and proficiency in the performance
3. The mutuality of respect and encouragement raises the level of creative input, excitement, and innovation

This feedback from the company was unambiguous in respect to the above creating a "community" or "family" feeling.

How they approach their craft has many lessons learned for commercial enterprise leaders. The scary truth based upon **Discussion Partners** advisory experience is, for the most part, global leaders are slow learners.

The five principles that we often see in tutorials on collaboration were present in the experience and are not surprising in their substance:

- Clarity Regarding Roles
- Exhaustive Preparation
- Mutual Trust
- Creative Input Encouraged Regardless of Tenure
- Shared Mindset for Success Delineation

What the experience did underscore based upon our collective experience is that in collaborative processes <u>EGO IS THE ENEMY</u>!!

If not, why are we so challenged in the commercial sector to achieve collaboration beyond lip service and generous self-serving interpretations of the word!

Most compelling in the Pilobolus experience was that for collaboration to be achieved as a shared mindset, egos must be minimized, engagement maximized, respect optimized and mutual trust achieved.

Among many of life's mysteries, one that hopefully we can resolve soon, and Pilobolus has, is how to translate the abstract thinking as to how collaboration can be achieved … moving it to reality from aspiration.

The *Inflection Point* is the lesson learned for those who want to focus on their passion … presume interdependence not independence! As important is the promotion of collaboration as a multi-generational fulcrum for direction and evaluation of success.

Chapter 5

Collapsing is Preferable!
(Tom)

To be successful regardless of which career path one chooses to pursue, there is a need to realistically assess the environment in which one wants to situate.

To that end, as the pace of emergence from the global recession accelerates, many companies are asking "Now what do I do?" (It is not only individuals) in order to address the following strategic questions:

1. How do I grow revenues concomitant with appropriate profit maximization?
2. How do I 'replenish' my critical mass of executives and others at a pace aligned with growth (raise the average IQ)?
3. How do I insure that the levels of employee engagement are differentiators in that your employees are and will remain "highly committed?"

4. How do I accelerate the introduction of innovation by first being hypercritical of pedestrian ideas?

5. How do I create a dashboard of key analytics that allow the enterprise to anticipate problems and adapt more quickly to changing conditions?

6. How do I channel the energies of those who have decided the enterprise being created is the most suitable platform to showcase their talents AND believe that affiliation with the company is worth the risk?

In our client work, Discussion Partners Collaborative has been urging consideration of three concepts in addressing the above:

1. **Apply the concept of the Null Hypothesis**: Assume you're mistaken in your planning assumptions and have disciplined contingency plans ready to employ on an as needed basis.

2. **Always be Recruiting while Selectively Hiring**: Similar to the sentiment expressed in the recent **HBR** article *Hire Slow Fire Fast,* we are encouraging our clients to focus, not on filling slots, but to interview on an on-going basis to (a.) gather marketplace intelligence, (b.) build up inventory of possible candidates, and (c.) reduce significantly the time to fill for critical positions.

3. **Collapse Around The Core**: Our working hypothesis is an extension of Jim Collin's philosophy of "first get the right people on the bus and in the right seats" in that we are encouraging a worst case leadership model for the present vs. being used as an 'in case' alternative.

CAC Principles

- Know who are your best people regardless of organizational hierarchy.
- Disrupt the career stage model in favor of time bound, fluid assignments and role architecture.
- Keep score on inputs and outcomes. What has the employee done? And how did the person acquire knowledge that allowed for their more than incremental contribution to operational performance?
- Think divorce not therapy. If the realistic assessment is that it is not going to work, call the question vs. taking time to avoid the inevitable, thereby running the risk of reputational diminishment for executives due to perceived indecisiveness.
- Think special ops vs. en masse interdictions … embed speed, agility, and interdependency into planning initiatives

The work **DPC** has been prosecuting regarding the above is embryonic. We are avoiding signature nomenclature such as "change management," "transformation," etc. as too static an approach given marketplace dynamics.

Alternatively, we are stating (a.) Disaggregate the enterprise plan into multiple strategic intents, (b.) Assign your best people regardless of hierarchy with a philosophy of high risk, high reward, (c.) Hold them accountable for achieving ambitious results and sharing how they did it, and (d.) If they aren't successful accelerate, the decision to demote, reassign, or displace.

To date our 18 month experience reinforces our working hypothesis that "Collapsing" the leadership and execution model has merit as the measurable results have been gratifying.

The *Inflection Point* is the awareness of the type of environment in which one would excel. To that end, there should be an effort made to appreciate that organizations are not static and they constantly reinvent themselves; the harnessing of the positive energy associated with this process can be of directional influence.

Chapter 6

To Plan Or Not To Plan!
(Tom)

Decades ago I went to a movie where one of the characters made the statement, "We Indians have a saying … no matter where you go, there you are."

Over the years I thought this statement was philosophically reassuring, but strategically idiotic! I validated this with my son-in-law, Neil, who is of Sioux descent. He responded, "Custer would have won if that was the belief."

As we contemplate "inflection points," it is best to think in terms of having a plan … if not every option will look great! Therein lies the risk.

One of my former colleagues from Arthur D. Little is an expert in strategic planning. After working at McKinsey and ADL, he went on to a distinguished career in multiple enterprises.

Over his career, he collected a series of planning principles that I thought you may find interesting.

- Your failure to plan does not constitute an emergency on my part. (Anonymous)
- All plans are firm until changed. (Steve Key)
- Miracles performed immediately ... the impossible takes a little longer. (Anonymous)
- If you don't know where you are going ... any road will take you there. (Lewis Carroll)
- Plan the work and work the plan. (Anonymous)
- Where there is no vision the people perish. (Proverbs 29:18)
- I believe in plans big enough to meet a situation which we can't possibly foresee now. (Harry Truman)
- Those who plan do better than those who do not plan even though they rarely stick to their plan. (Winston Churchill)
- Plans are worthless. Planning is essential. (Dwight Eisenhower)
- A goal not written is a wish. (Anonymous)
- Goals are dreams we convert to meet plans and take actions to fulfill. (Ziglar)
- By failing to prepare you are preparing to fail. (Benjamin Franklin)

The *Inflection Point* that has to be addressed ... without a plan can best hope for a reply of "there you are!" Irony aside, a process of reflective discourse has limited outlet unless and until it embeds consideration as to what would be the venue for one to showcase their talents and channel their energies most successfully. As important is the role enterprises play in de-risking the self-discovery journey.

Chapter 7

They Lost Us At Paperclip!
(Tom)

As we enter the North American and European summer and scramble for the perfect swimsuit to hide the largesse of the winter, it is helpful to reinforce the issue that an outstanding customer experience is sometimes less about the product, but more about the level of service that supports the transaction.

In the context of Inflection Points, it is advisable to focus on the realization that for every action there is a consequence, and for every consequence for those willing to accept control of their life, there is a need to recognize life's choices are yours to make.

There is an oft repeated line from the Jerry McGuire movie: "You had me at hello."

Unfortunately, I have an alternative less glowing rejoinder based upon an experience with a former cable company: "They lost me at Paperclip!"

Several months ago, on a Sunday night, our TV started acting up in a manner that clearly indicated a problem with the provider.

Unfortunately, this episode was in addition to diminished capability at predictable hours and the fact that the wireless capacity seemed to run out of steam if it had to climb stairs!

On the above two issues we had the "tech" out several times with no discernible improvements.

The problem with the TV however was new!

We called our provider and asked for some assistance. They told us in order for them to help "first you will have to put a paperclip into the cable box!"

We were stunned on two levels: (a.) These days of high technology, why should the effectiveness of a machine rely on a paperclip and (b.) In the world of e-files, did we even have a paperclip?

Turns out we did … and got the TV back … eventually, but the ridiculousness of the situation had been dormant in our memory.

It resurfaced when, to avoid looking ridiculous to grandchildren, we bought a larger TV. The retailer and installers both indicated that the cable box was "old style," and our provider had a new model, which had become available recently.

Ever hopeful, we went to get this new model with the objectives that not only would the picture be better … but other deficiencies would be mitigated.

You have to envision going to a provider in a strip mall, whose offices look like they were created when *Leave it to Beaver* was a hit! When we asked the service rep for particulars on the capability of the new machine, she was clueless. Her response was, "The new one is more high tech."

I resisted asking, "So now we don't need paperclips?" But, instead, we focused on the capabilities of the new machine in the context of our problems. Again we heard "high tech!" We probed again. "What does that mean?" and got mostly a befuddled stare ... to the point where we walked out.

Within two hours, out of frustration and hopefulness, we switched providers ...

At the moment, we are not certain if that was the correct move. We only know continuing with a "high tech" machine, which apparently does not require us to have a paperclip handy, seems the wiser course.

The *Inflection Point,* **beyond not throwing away all of your paperclips, is that there is no logic or reason to accept the status quo in any form The challenging of assumptions is advisable and the pivot point for determination of risk.**

Chapter 8

Don't Ask Do Tell!
(Tom)

This Chapter was written the evening of February 1ˢᵗ, the day of the Super Bowl.

The authors felt it was illustrative, given the choices made, to remind readers of one of the critical questions ... How do you want to be remembered?

Being Boston-based, with the Super Bowl imminent, a number of questions are being raised by our New England clients ...

Not least among them is the issue of "Deflategate," given the extensive media exposure, conflicting with the loyalty New Englanders feel towards the Patriots and their over a decade long of professionalism and success.

On to safer and/or saner topics, there are two other Boston based "sports incidents" that provide insights for commercial companies.

In January 2002, during the AFC Championship game, there was a blizzard much more modest than the one we are currently experiencing in Boston; it is euphemistically referred to as "The Snow Bowl."

During the game's final moments, Bill Belichick asked Adam Vinatieri if he could kick a field goal from the then distance to win the game ...

Vinatieri answered truthfully "no."

Later, the Patriots got closer, Vinatieri did kick a field goal, and they went on to win the Super Bowl the next month.

We are left to ponder, given his undeniable skills and self-confidence, what would have happened if he had said yes and missed?

Bostonians have an alternative situation that did not have a happy ending.

In 2003, during the seventh game for the American League pennant, the then pitcher, Pedro Martinez, got into trouble and was asked by manager, Grady Little, if he wanted to pitch to the next hitter.

Martinez said yes and gave up a hit that later sealed the game for the Yankees.

So to the point ...

Belichick knew he would get a straight answer from Vinatieri, the example of "Do Tell" the truth vs. worry about personal implications.

Little knew, or should have, that NO was not in Martinez's DNA and should never have asked the question in the first place ... the example of "Don't Ask."

In the commercial sector, leaders tend to forget sometimes that ego, proficiency, and circumstances have to be in alignment for success to be achieved.

It would be helpful if we, as mangers, were constantly mindful of the proficiencies of our associates and never asked anyone an aspirational question unless we were certain we would get an objective and sincere answer.

Important to our decision making process: Uninformed and unsupportive people, ostensibly there to be of assistance, should NEVER be compensated when their services are found wanting!

The Patriots went on to win number 4! The question now becomes one of reflective legacy: Will this remarkable achievement be remembered or tainted by the controversy of Deflategate?

The *Inflection Point* is the awareness that one's reputation is timeless ... given social media ... the question becomes can you direct awareness or is it a casualty of circumstances? The adage *you are how you were* ... is appropriate.

Chapter 9

Your Tool Should Work ... But You Should Also Know How To Use It! (Sean)

My initial instinct was to put my car into reverse and drive back to my parent's house as I sat outside a Veterans Affairs (VA) center near Philadelphia. I was to have my first face-to-face mental health counseling session with someone who I had only spoken to over the phone. Yet, I knew that the previous nine months of despair, confusion and frustration had placed me at this precipice. Either I could retreat back into a life that didn't meet my expectations, but one I just couldn't escape, or I could leap out into a world where I allowed others to help me.

In the previous nine months, anxiety's grip had twisted my chest so tight that I fantasized about trading my body in for a new one. Up to that point, I thought I had no control over the physical torture my body was enduring. Days became tediously long hours filled with waves of vibrations coursing through my system. These weren't the ones the Beach Boys sang about, but swells of dread manifested from any sort of external stimuli. I had returned from my second deployment to Iraq and was attempting to transition, again, back into the civilian world.

At first, I was able to maintain an outward appearance of normal; however, the cap I had on these intense emotions slowly began to disintegrate. "Is everything okay?" people would ask me. The inner turmoil began to bubble to the surface as my facial expressions consistently showed worry, intensity, and fear. My once compassionate and patient nature dwindled as I grew easily and intensely frustrated with people close to me over the simplest of things. Doubt, an unfamiliar word to me up to that point in my internal vocabulary, accompanied every thought, decision, or interaction— my entire perspective of life itself. I had once led men in combat, and now, the most mundane decisions riddled me with crumbling worry.

The juxtaposition of what I was and what I had become filled me with embarrassment. How could an educated, trained, and capable man not find a solution himself? Avoidance became my coping mechanism as I stepped away from work, hobbies and any meaningful personal relationship that I had. The interpersonal interactions within those spheres only reminded me of how far gone I was. However, there must have been some glimmer of hope because I found myself researching mental health professionals, which brought me to the Department of Veterans Affairs website. I didn't fully understand how the influences of my combat experiences had on my current state, but knowing that there were readily available and free mental health professionals at my disposal was enough for me to make a phone call.

I called the center to seek more information. I was forwarded to Allison, one of the counselors at the center. I explained to her, at least the best that I could, the details of my current state, and how I wanted to start counseling as soon as possible. I also explained that I wasn't living in the immediate area, but was moving closer to the vet center in six weeks to live with my parents. She explained that it was against policy for the center to conduct phone sessions. This comment made me sink even further as I thought about another bureaucratic policy being a roadblock to my infant journey towards betterment.

The curdling agony starting its brew inside my gut was immediately extinguished when she said that she understood the desperate state I was in, and she would gladly do weekly sessions over the phone until I was settled in Pennsylvania. What? Was this someone, whom I've never met, willing to bend the rules to help me? Was this someone who put the betterment of the individual above the stacks of regulations? I can't speak for Allison, but this was how I interpreted her actions that day, and can't quite describe the sliver of hope that opened within me after hearing those words.

Over the next few weeks, Allison and I spoke over the phone. FYI—I'm a bit of a talker. The phone sessions were a blur as I dumped years of stories, thoughts, theories and emotions through the receiver. Allison would meet me with understanding and patience as she allowed me to vent, which I later understood as her way of getting to know me—to understand all the variables associated with how I ended up becoming one of her clients.

She was a service member herself, and she was able to identify with the unique nature of military life—all its wonderfulness, contradictions, camaraderie, pain and thrill. There was also a practical side to these sessions. Allison explained to me how the cognitive therapy process worked, which satisfied my analytical need to understand a system that created results. Finally, she provided a neutral and nonjudgmental outlet for me where I didn't have to worry about whether I looked too weak or would be embarrassed about what I was feeling.

This brings us back to the beginning of my story. What I've learned is that mental health improvement does not follow a linear path where you start off in one state and gradually get better. It's a process that webs in many directions, filled with progress and setbacks, and small victories and defeats. Sitting outside the vet center waiting to meet Allison for the first time in person, the same feelings of dread and anxiety billowed in stomach and chest. I could've easily driven away, never to have any further communication with them. There was no external consequence if I chose to not continue, no fines, ridicule, loss of pay, no responsibility to others. There was only the internal consequence where I ignored my sole responsibility—to take care of myself.

Only in six weeks was she able to show me that taking care of oneself isn't weak, but something that's necessary. You're only good to others when you've made self-care a priority. Allison showed me that we're capable of altering our perspective—it just takes time, effort, and a willingness to give oneself over to the process.

I opened my car door, walked up the flight of stairs, opened the door to the vet center and was greeted by Allison. We've been meeting for almost three and a half years. Through the acute training and experience she's received by being a VA counselor, she's been able to address my issues stemming from post-traumatic stress. She's given me homework to do, which keeps me actively engaged with my therapy between sessions. She's assisted me in getting registered with the VA medical health system—exposing me to benefits I didn't even know I was eligible for as a combat veteran. Allison was my prime advocate when filing for disability once I was diagnosed as having PTS.

The partnership that we've developed is based upon trust and the willingness we both have to come to the table ready to get to work. She's always demonstrated an incredibly high standard of professionalism, expertise, compassion, and patience. I learned that it was my responsibility to be honest and candid while we had our sessions, and to do the work between sessions she requested of me.

My VA experiences have taught me that the road to improvement can't be done by others. The veteran has to be an active participant. I was once consumed with so much anxiety I felt I was completely paralyzed. The VA provided me an outlet to begin to take action—to take control of my life with the help and guidance of professionals that work within the system. I understand the system isn't perfect and there should always be an ongoing process of accountability and improvement. But the sense of empowerment the professionals at the VA have shown me has been life altering. The VA won't carry you down the path, but will certainly help guide you in a more positive direction. I still actively seek opportunities for self-improvement or care. I don't view opportunities like counseling as necessary, but rather as life enhancers. I'm a different man.

The *Inflection Point* is that being uncomfortable is not only a good thing, but necessary to advance in any endeavor. Paralysis caused by anxiety or the unwillingness to endure periods of physical or emotional discomfort is psychologically and physically damaging. Being uncomfortable is unpleasant, but remember that part of that feeling encompasses the beginning moments of momentum towards whatever you're after.

Chapter 10

A Talking Point's Unintended Effect (Sean)

"Twenty-two veterans commit suicide every day," says the talking point originating from a Department of Veterans Affairs report on veteran suicides. This figure has become the mantra from politicians to advocacy groups, and persists in many of the social and professional circles in which I circulate. The rhetorical repetition of this figure has deluded the context in which it originates. If you bring up troops or veterans, you get more ink—not a revolutionary tactic, but still effective in U.S. culture. Also, having prominent defense officials label it an 'epidemic' narrows how the topic is framed and referenced in public discourse.

What if I were to tell you that someone in the United States dies from suicide every 12.8 minutes? Shocked? Well, did you know that suicide is the 10th leading cause of death in the United States? Dumbfounded? I certainly was when doing research about suicide for a graduate school project. The American Foundation for Suicide Prevention provides these references based on 2013 data from the Center for Disease Control, which tracks mortality rates including suicide. Is there a frenzy of advocacy groups, policy makers, and other stakeholders beating the drums about the U.S. suicide epidemic?

That last question is rhetorical and included to prove a point; who and how a story is framed plays a significant role in how far said story travels. Mass distribution of a story also relies on the credibility of the source in the minds of audiences. When that credible source, or sources, has a powerful platform, the amplification and penetration of a singular angle of a story's narrative creates objective truth in the minds of audiences. Messages become even more embedded when audiences are only partially listening, or have minimal familiarity in the subject matter being discussed. Yet, each and everyone one of you knows complexities of the personal, professional and social worlds each of you exists within can't be simplified by a few talking points.

Humans will piece together received information to construct an internal narrative. These narratives help us understand our world by creating our perceived notions of reality. Even when more accurate information is received, we have a challenging time altering our existing internal narrative. Recent wars in Iraq and Afghanistan created a tendency to associate all discussions about veterans with members from this younger generation who've served during these wars. This is why when the topic of veteran suicide appears, audiences conjure images of current service members or younger veterans succumbing to the act. The reality is the majority of reported veteran suicides are by members 50 years old or older. I'm under the belief there wouldn't be as much attention focused on veteran suicide if audiences couldn't connect statistics in context with the most current generation of veterans. Here's an example of how the framing of a story at a macro-level, despite existing conflicting information, strongly influences how our society creates perceptions of a given subgroup.

This chapter isn't about cognitive processing or sociology, but bear with me as I present another sociological theory—the "Looking Glass Self," which brings us to a micro-level. Early 20th Century sociologist Charles Horton Cooley's concept is widely accepted in current psychology and sociology. It states our individual sense of self relies on our interactions with our social world. In other words, we construct our inner narrative about who we are from how we believe others think of us. This theory explains body image issues, peer pressure, and a host of other sociological phenomena.

Throughout my personal transition out of active duty, I received much praise and congratulation, along observing an underlying sympathy beneath the celebratory phrases. My perception of this sympathy morphed into perceived pity as veteran mental health issues associated with post-traumatic stress, veteran unemployment, and veteran suicide filled much of my professional and personal channels of communication. I began to view our veteran community, including myself, as damaged. The overarching narrative about young veterans in the United States seemed to support this. Those who have the resources to influence public perceptions, also referred to as opinion leaders, shaped the narrative, which influenced my belief that the greater society held this perception of veterans. I began to believe that's who I was—damaged goods.

A military experience provides ample opportunities for individuals to feel empowered, to feel a consistent presence of purpose. Much of the issues related to deficiencies in veteran's welfare are that their new civilian environments lack sufficient access to opportunities to feel purposeful. Add an ominous social perception that you're viewed as negatively afflicted, and that veteran has an even bleaker view of their status in life.

The above description is something I personally experienced, and it was a recipe for an extended period of stagnation. Simply put—I believed the hype. What brought me out of utter paralysis was my exposure to empowerment. These opportunities come in the form of veterans groups whose mission is to build community and camaraderie among the veteran population. We're able to get solid footing on a slippery path. An altered perspective in a supportive environment swept away the dark clouds that billowed around me. I realized how much authority was at my disposal simply by altering the external influences I exposed myself to.

Veteran welfare advocates have brought to the forefront important issues that merit dialogue and action. However, the voracity of these efforts can have unintentional consequences. At a certain point individuals have to transition from problem identifiers to problem solvers.

The _Inflection Point_ is we have the power to alter our perspectives on any given situation. The alteration doesn't mean being naïve and keeping your head in the sand. It's imperative to take personal responsibility in changing the narrative towards a story that yields positive personal and social outcomes.

Chapter 11

Continuity Planning Myth-Ready
Now Means Readiness
(Tom)

**EXECUTIVE
TRANSITIONS**
A Guide for Transitioning Executives and the Companies that Employ Them

Tom Casey and Karen Warlin
with
Sean Casey and Tobey Choate

We want to share with you some findings from the research that contributed to our recently published book (above) supported by our transition advisory work with over 400 executives since 2013.

In the delivery of our work to executives working on their post-employment plans, an area for dialogue is the "readiness" of their successors.

Early in our work, when we posed the question "Are your successors up for the challenge?" we frequently heard the response "no," "not yet," "not sure," or "hard to tell."

Initially advisors were somewhat cynical about the response as Type A personalities have healthy egos. However, when we dug deeper into the comments, a number of in-common concerns were articulated by our clients.

Essentially, they saw the 'deficiencies' or 'shortfalls' in the following areas:

Global Preparation: Given that most of the new wave of leadership began their careers during the recession of the late 80s and early 90s, the ability to secure an expatriate assignment, or participate in extensive international travel, had been curtailed. Moreover, the cost constraint mentality that existed discouraged pan-organizational initiatives in favor of 'home grown' strategic intents. Thus, the ability to learn more about global challenges was truncated.

Collaboration: The above also has to be put into the context of "how we now collaborate." Since the late 90s collaboration has devolved to a state of electronic touch points.

The days when mission focused teams were created and participants entered a room prepared to persuade others to their point of view are waning. The use of electronic communication is now the norm. A compelling example, of course, is Facebook as a principal communication vehicle. This type of interface can be extrapolated easily to implications for collaborative efforts.

Written Communication: As a rapidly aging baby boomer, I still remember the Palmer Method, the nuns' obsession with good grammar, and living in dreaded fear that my mother, a master's prepared English teacher, would want to review my homework.

Having survived the above, I do look askance at the quality of writing that is offered today.

We have become executives who believe that well-presented PowerPoint decks are the bastion of good communication and the more graphics the more forceful the argument.

The art of creating a persuasive paragraph, to be incorporated into a white paper or education treatise, has suffered according to our clients.

Intellectual Curiosity: Most Boomer CEOs are voracious readers of biographies. In addition to reading books about or written by Jack Welch, they focus on political biographies.

To reinforce the point, the acceptance of books by Doris Kearns Goodwin on Lincoln (*Team of Rivals*), and Roosevelt/Taft (*The Bloody Pulpit*) are offered.

Twice a year **Discussion Partners** creates a reading list for our C-Suite clients based upon the books they are focused on at the time.

What we learned through this initiative was that the C-Suite wants to understand "how past leaders dealt with adversity."

Our clients' concern is that this lack of "wanting to understand" is of secondary importance to domain expertise.

The above 'concerns' do not detract from the comprehensive work being done on succession planning efforts. Moreover, our clients would also stipulate that the above should be embedded into the planning process. The observations of our clients suggest, a need to be aware that if the lack of opportunity and/or focus of the incoming wave of leaders is perceived as problematic, an organized response should be forthcoming.

The key *Inflection Point* is the need to presume that the proficiencies that most perceive as crucial may have passed their "sell by date." There is a need to constantly rejuvenate one's skills in order to be optimally positioned to exploit desired directions.

Chapter 12

Inflection Point Conclusions

It is very difficult to look for symmetry between and among the experiences and beliefs of three separate authors. This is particularly challenging given the diversity of ages, experiences, and developmental platforms for each contributor. However disparate our origin, there is <u>congruence</u> on points of view regarding *Inflection Points.*

Threshold

These are the 'top 6' **influencers** the authors suggest be considered as the 'baseline' in that all humans walking the planet have to contend with their implications:

- **Age:** We are all aging from the moment we are born! The **influencer** is not how we feel about age, but how we cope with the process ranging from obsession over implications to disregard, looking forward without allowing distraction.

- **Relationships**: Spousal, parental, children, familial, and extended, are all material **influencers** in that no one has ever been universally loved, respected, or admired. The question is your comfort with how you are perceived by those who matter to you, concomitant to the comfort you feel with your level of effort to enjoin positive relationships.

- **Means**: "Greed is good" is the famous utterance of Gordon Gecko in *Wall Street*. There are those who have too much month left at the end of their money, those who have only month, and those who have lost track of how wealthy they are fortunate enough to have become. The **influencer** is one's level of security. Bill and Melinda Gates are the most visible representatives among many others who have decided to share their good fortune. There are others who live day to day in search of stability. For the most part, we all aspire to our own definition of 'sufficiency' … the level of comfort we have feeling comfortable.

- **Location**: Whereby your location is in fact its own **influencer**. The truth of the matter is that the words 'safety and security' are now goals vs. givens. Regardless of your source of news, there is an onslaught of grim reminders. The ability to cope is the pertinent determinant as to how one leverages, adapts, or succumbs to this element.

- **Societal**: With all of its benefits, the US is in a state of turmoil on two key elements of foundational support, health care and education; some other societies are in better, others are in worse shape on these issues. The authors believe the **influencers** selected are the most influential criteria for foundational purposes.

- **Enterprise**: De-risking is an enterprise obligation. Regardless of what study or article you review, the unambiguous conclusion is that in great companies the pursuit of this strategic intent is relentless and material as individuals ponder the "now what?"

Accelerators

As the authors review the compilation of writings centered around what are and are not **influencers**, and mindful of the above, we have selected our 'top 3' we perceive drive one towards taking risks, devoting sufficient energy and objectively appraising progress.

The "core" of coming to an *Inflection Point* and controlling vs. being controlled by outcomes are *Realism, Focus, and Courage.*

There are, of course, others … however, for what it is worth, expanding on the above …

- **Sense of Self (Realism):** The ability one has to realistically appraise their proficiencies and short-comings leveraging the first and adapting to the second. This goes beyond aspiring to be successful or to be admired, to a focus of energy. Independent of the benefits bestowed on one … the fulcrum one needs to be mindful of is 'realism.'
- **Channeling (Focus):** Edison once espoused that successful creation was "one percent inspiration and ninety-nine percent perspiration." The noted philosopher Yogi Berra opined "When you come to the fork in the road … take it." The real questions before us are straightforward (a.) What do you want to ac-

complish? (b.) What is the directional roadmap for focusing energy? and (c.) The often overlooked "How will you know when you have arrived?" None of these are attainable unless or until one concentrates, avoids distractions, and commits to outcomes vs. wishes.

- **Relentlessness (Courage):** The authors pondered whether or not to label this attribute "dealing with rejection" ... but thought courage more acceptable. Regardless of labeling, our conclusion is that it takes a special trait, a drive if you will, to challenge the status quo, take sensible risks, and achieve results independent of setbacks and inevitable failures encountered during the journey.

Inflection Points Summary

Whether it is dealing with age, re-entry challenges post combat, or the desire to challenge societal norms and level of enterprise de-risking, pursuit of advancement are daunting. These *Inflection Points* compel proactive decision making as inertia can and likely will result if constantly asking oneself the question "what if?"

INFLECTION POINTS:
RISK READINESS & FEARLESS FAILURE

Chapter 1: The *Inflection Point* is the belief that the concept of reconciliation between and among age cohorts is a crucial awareness aspect to incorporate into decision-making and as a criterion for evaluation of success.

Chapter 2: The *Inflection Point* is the realization that life is not determined by actuarial tables, it is the focus of what one does and why, concomitant with the satisfaction of resultant choices.

Chapter 3: The *Inflection Point* is the realization that family orientation is THE essential foundation for decision-making. The direction that can be provided can be useful or less than … the key is to recognize that your choices are YOUR CHOICES!

Chapter 4: The *Inflection Point* is the awareness that societal norms are in and of themselves often challenging. Granted we are using Peru as an example, but the "glass ceiling" is alive and well in many societies. Our hypothesis is that assertive risk taking, regardless of level of support, is the provenance of the individual and self-accountability the foundation for success.

Chapter 5: The *Inflection Point* is the awareness of the type of environment in which one would excel. To that end, there should be an effort made to appreciate that organizations are not static and they constantly reinvent themselves; the harnessing of the positive energy associated with this process can be of directional influence.

Chapter 6: The *Inflection Point* that has to be addressed … without a plan can best hope for a reply of "there you are!" Irony aside, a process of reflective discourse has limited outlet unless and until it embeds consideration as to what would be the venue for one to showcase their talents and channel their energies most successfully. As important is the role enterprises play in de-risking the self-discovery journey.

Chapter 7: The *Inflection Point*, beyond not throwing away all of your paperclips, is that there is no logic or reason to accept the status quo in any form The challenging of assumptions is advisable and the pivot point for determination of risk.

Chapter 8: The *Inflection Point* is the awareness that one's reputation is timeless … given social media … the question becomes can you direct awareness or is it a casualty of circumstances? The adage you are how you were ... is appropriate.

Chapter 9: The *Inflection Point* is that being uncomfortable is not only a good thing, but necessary to advance in any endeavor. Paralysis caused by anxiety or the unwillingness to endure periods of physical or emotional discomfort is psychologically and physically damaging. Being uncomfortable is unpleasant, but remember that part of that feeling encompasses the beginning moments of momentum towards whatever you're after.

Chapter 10: The key *Inflection Point* is the need to presume that the proficiencies that most perceive as crucial may have passed their "sell by date." There is a need to constantly rejuvenate one's skills in order to be optimally positioned to exploit desired directions.

About the Authors

Tom Casey is the Managing Principal of Discussion Partner Collaborative LLC (www.discussionpartners.com). DPC is a global executive advisory firm focused on Organization Design and Leadership Effectiveness. An expert in the development of Transformation and Transition strategies, consulting in over 20 countries during his 35-year career, Tom held senior level positions with Harbridge House Inc., Arthur D. Little, PricewaterhouseCoopers, Buck Consultants, and The Concours Group before founding Discussion Partners. He has authored over 300 books, articles, and four books including two best sellers. Tom is a retired Special Operations Officer serving in both the United States Air Force and Army. He holds a Bachelor's Degree from the University of Alaska and MA and MBA degrees from Rivier University, also graduating from the Yale School of Management Executive Program. Tom can be reached at tcasey@dpcadvisors.com

Sean Casey is a major in the U.S. military with two combat tours in Iraq. Sean is pursuing a career in professional communications, and is presently working as a public relations consultant. Sean holds a bachelor's degree in political science from Miami University (Ohio) and a master's degree in public communication from Drexel University. He is the author of the blog *Sean Maybe Heard* and was a contributor to one of Tom Casey's best sellers. Sean can be reached at seanmaybeheard@gmail.com or via Twitter: @seancasey442

Ariana Pazos Aramburú is a Research Advisor with Discussion Partner Collaborative LLC and Senior Process Consultant in Travex Security, a partner of the American Express Travel Network. Ariana graduated from Universidad del Pacifico in Lima, Peru. She will be attending the MBA program at the HAAS School of Business University of California Berkeley in September. Ariana can be reached at arianapazosaramburu@gmail.com.

References

[i] Booz and Company, *The Third Billion*

[ii] GMI Ratings, 2013

[iii] Planig (Plan Nacional de Igualdad y Género) 2012 (2010 Statistics)

[iv] Interview with 10 Peruvian female executives